DAVID T. LITTLE

JACKIE ARIAS

for Mezzo-Soprano and Piano

from the opera *JFK*

Libretto by
ROYCE VAVREK

HENDON MUSIC

BOOSEY & HAWKES

DISTRIBUTED BY

HAL•LEONARD®

7777 W. BLUEMOUND RD. P.O. BOX 13819 MILWAUKEE, WI 53213

www.boosey.com
www.halleonard.com

The opera JFK *commissioned by*
Fort Worth Opera, Darren K. Woods, General Director;
American Lyric Theater, Lawrence Edelson, Producing Artistic Director;
l'Opéra de Montréal

Commission underwritten by Linda H. & Richard N. Claytor, Ph.D.
for Sophie.

Premiered by Fort Worth Opera
at Bass Performance Hall, Fort Worth, TX on April 23, 2016
Steven Osgood, conductor

JACKIE ARIAS

Jackie Arias
from *JFK*

Libretto by
ROYCE VAVREK

DAVID T. LITTLE
(2016)

Midnight is the Loneliest Hour

[JACKIE is crowned in moonlight, sitting by the window, smoking her cigarette.]

979-0-051-80217-3

Printed 2018

* For performance of excerpts, chorus can be omitted.

You Shiver

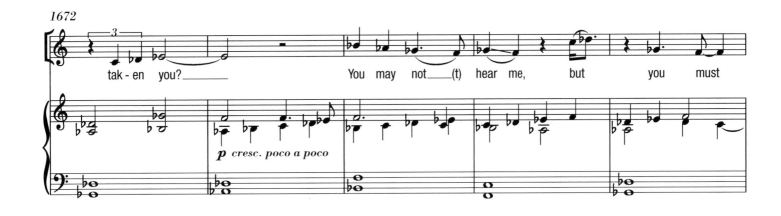

hear me out._____

I shut my eyes,__ co - ver my ears, my heart in shreds,

at the sug - gest - ion, the mere__ sug - gest - ion, of oth - er__

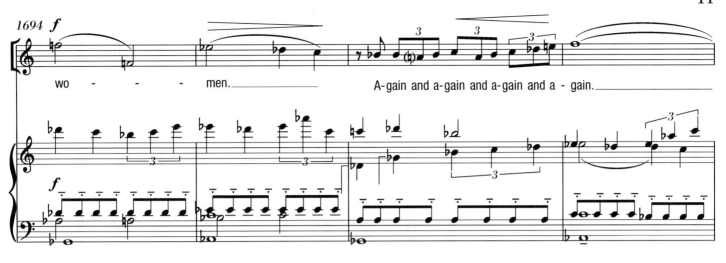

wo - - - men.____ A-gain and a-gain and a-gain and a - gain.____

rit. ($\boldsymbol{\downarrow} = \boldsymbol{55}$)

A - gain and a-gain and a-gain and a - gain.____

[JACK's eyes open, unseen by JACKIE,
but the audience is privy.]

1702 $\boldsymbol{\downarrow} = \boldsymbol{72}$

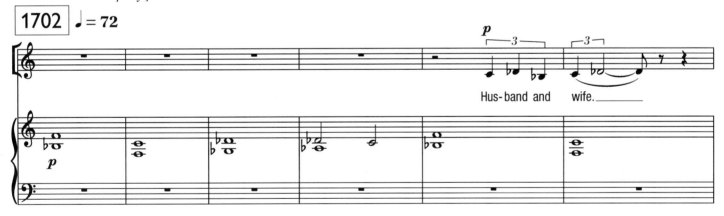

Hus-band and wife.____

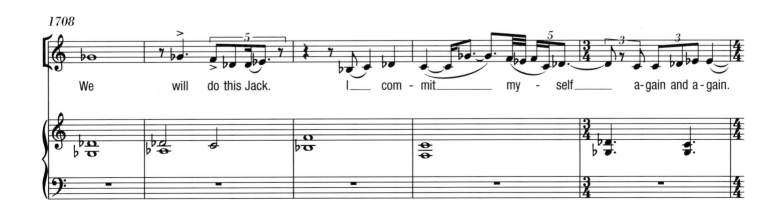

We will do this Jack. I____ com - mit____ my - self____ a-gain and a - gain.

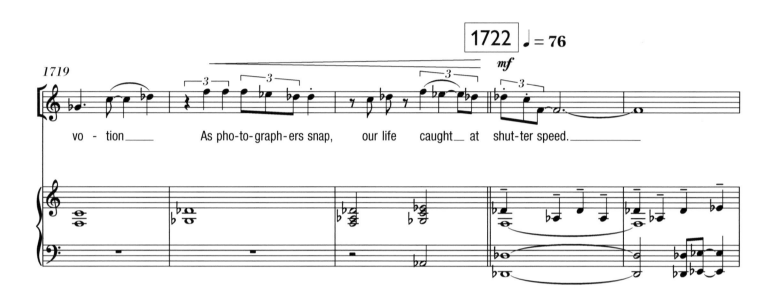

love you. I re-com-mit with great hope.

[JACKIE sinks into the bed with JACK. Hopefully she is now able to sleep. In the hallway CLARA pushes her maid's cart and RATHBONE stands guard. THEY sing together.]

[JACKIE sinks into the bed with JACK. Hopefully she is now able to sleep. In the hallway CLARA pushes her maid's cart and RATHBONE stands guard.]

1750 meno mosso (♩ = 72)

* Suggested ending: add fermata to final beat of this bar, or simply resolve to A♭ major on the downbeat of m1762.

Won't You Touch Me (Mask, Shield, Armor, Crown)

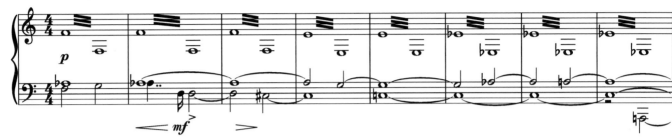

[SHE reaches out to touch the painting, the painted girl animates, giggles, squirms away.]

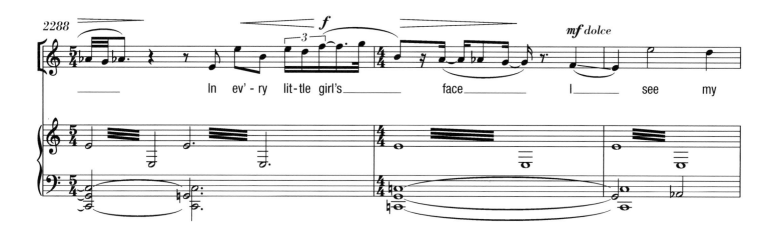

In ev'-ry lit-tle girl's face I see my

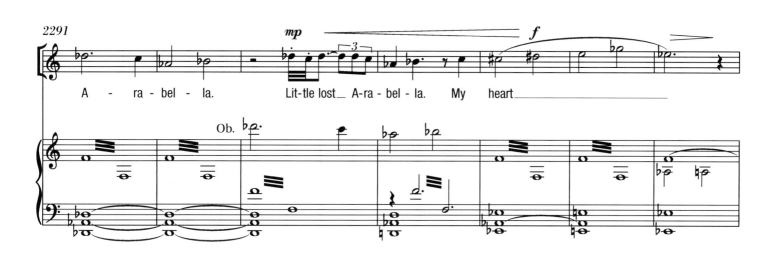

A - ra - bel - la. Lit-tle lost A-ra - bel - la. My heart

skips. Won't you touch me? Let your lit-tle fin- gers ex-plore my face.

Won't you touch me? Scratch my cheek. Press in - to my eyes.

f as if in slow motion

B. Choir

The

CUE: sing only if Boys' Choir needs support;
subsets okay at the discretion of the conductor.
Should not be seen to be singing, only heard.

mp as if in slow motion
senza vib., like a boys' choir

S.

The

CUE: sing only if Boys' Choir needs support;
subsets okay at the discretion of the conductor.
Should not be seen to be singing, only heard.

A.

Cl.

p   L.

[JACKIE starts walking, making her way in front of the TEXAS BOYS CHOIR,
searching their faces for the features of her son, PATRICK.]

2307

eyes of Te - xas are u - pon you. The eyes of

B. Choir

f as if in slow motion

The eyes of Te - xas are u - pon you. The eyes

S.

eyes of Te - xas are u - pon you. The eyes of

senza vib., like a Boys' Choir
mp as if in slow motion

A.

The eyes of Te - xas are u - pon you. The eyes

Vla. trem.

mf   p

* For performance of excerpts, chorus can be omitted.

Let me moth - - - er____ you...____

____ you...____ In ev'ry lit-tle boy's____ face_ I_ see my Pat - rick.

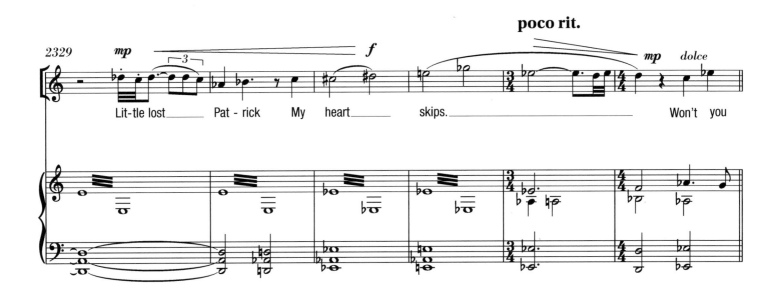

Lit-tle lost____ Pat - rick My heart____ skips.____ Won't you

2335 ♩ = 60 subito

touch me? Let your lit-tle fin - gers___ ex-plore my face. Won't you touch me?

[From behind a scrim, the CHORUS OF
CHILDLESS MOTHERS are illuminated.]

2340

2341 ♩ = 54 - 56

Scratch my cheek. Press in - to my eyes.

as CHORUS OF CHILDLESS MOTHERS

mp weary

S. I wear my mask, my shield, my ar - mor.

as CHORUS OF CHILDLESS MOTHERS

mp weary

A. I wear my mask, my shield, my ar - mor.

f ⟨ ⟩ *mp*

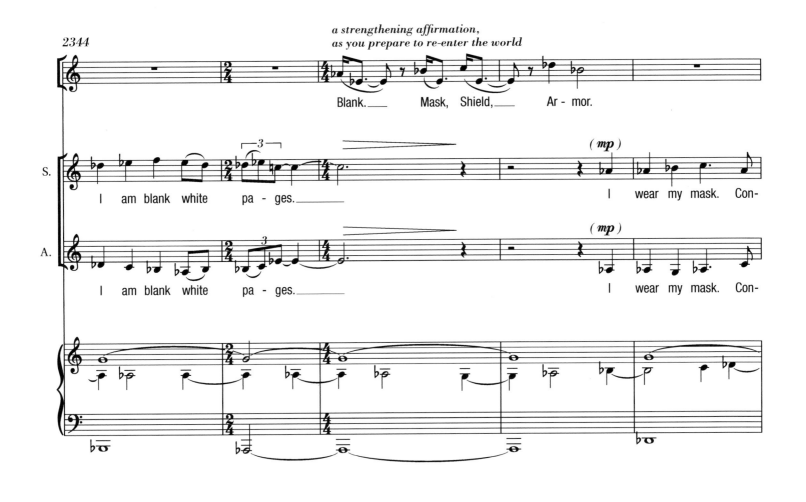

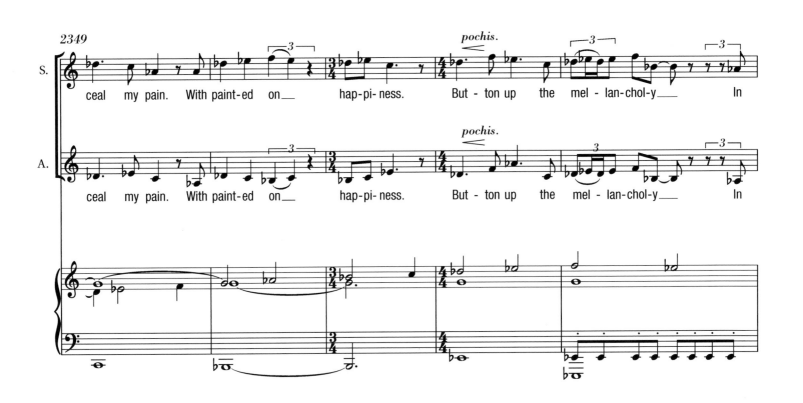

[CLARA moves toward JACKIE preparing to place the
hat on her head, JACKIE'S final preparation for the
day. JACKIE ascends to the dais.]

2364

[JACKIE places the pillbox hat on her head and enters the banquet hall as the room erupts in applause and excitement.]

2367

Blank. Mask. Shield. Ar - mor. Mask. Shield. Ar - mor. My Crown.

B. Choir

you. The eyes of Te - xas are u - pon you.

_____ you. _____ The eyes _____ of Te - xas are u-pon_ you.

S.

you. The eyes of Te - xas are u - pon you.

A.

_____ you. _____ The eyes _____ of Te - xas are u - pon _ you.

2372

Timp. / Hp.

* Suggested ending: add a fermata at the end of this bar.